SOUTH AUSTRALIA

CHILDREN OF THE
DREAMTIME

CHILDREN OF THE
DREAMTIME

HELEN BALDWIN

EDITED BY LAURA MURRAY

NEW HOLLAND

To Michael and Lizzie

The author wishes to express her gratitude to John Skarratt for his photography of the artworks and Pat Ross for typing the original manuscript.

Published in 2021 by New Holland Publishers
First published in 1989 by Child & Associates Publishing Pty Ltd
Sydney • Auckland

Level 1, 178 Fox Valley Road, Wahroonga, NSW 2076, Australia
5/39 Woodside Ave, Northcote, Auckland 0627, New Zealand

newhollandpublishers.com

A record of this book is held at the British Library and the National Library of Australia.

ISBN 9781760793623

Group Managing Director: Fiona Schultz
Paintings selected and text edited by Laura Murray
Designer: Andrew Davies
Production Director: Arlene Gippert
Printed in China

Front cover: *Markilyi, Yuntjin and Nutji Nutji (Lizzie, Lucy and Emma)* Page 1: *Boys with Mandarins* Page 3: *Road to Mt Liebig, near Papunya* Page 5: *Tony at the Top* Back cover: *Women from Amata, Dancing, Yirara College Fete 1984*

10 9 8 7 6 5 4 3 2 1

Keep up with New Holland Publishers on Facebook
facebook.com/NewHollandPublishers

CONTENTS

INTRODUCTION

For several decades Helen Baldwin painted outback Australia and the Aboriginal people. Her travels took her throughout western New South Wales and to Alice Springs, Darwin, Yuendumu, Napperby, Mbunghara, Papunya, Kintore, Docker River, Areyonga, Maryvale and countless places in between. Through her friendship with Michael Ellis and his wife Lizzie, a full-blood Aborigine of the Ngaanatjarra tribe, Helen has been taken to special areas that few white people have ever seen.

The natural affinity for the Central Australian desert and its people felt by Helen is visible in her artistic work. She is able to see through the incongruous Western clothing, tangled hair and ubiquitous dust to the flame that gave birth to one of the purest forms of spirituality ever articulated. During the day, surrounded by the litter of modern mythology – crushed drink cans, empty wine flagons, rusting car bodies – the local Aboriginal people can appear broken in heart and spirit. At night, telling Dreamtime stories by the campfire, an ancient dignity lights the eyes of the old people.

To tribal Aboriginal people simple acts of daily life have spiritual significance. With few possessions beyond the requirements of physical survival – temporary shelters, spears, digging sticks and wooden dishes – these people wandered for 60 000 years or more across Australia. The earth and stones, rivers, trees and waterholes, animals, birds, plants, moon and stars yielded up their secrets and became part of tribal life through ceremonies that answered eternal questions of creation, birth and death. Paintings, music and dance gave expression to the ceremonial stories.

At one time all Aboriginal art was sacred, although not all was secret. Some paintings were descriptive, showing the people food gathering, story telling or journeying to a new camp site. Special paintings and ritual objects were hidden and viewed only by certain tribal members during important ceremonies. These were ephemeral, often lasting no longer than the ceremony for which they were made. The message, not the medium, was sacred.

It is the essence of this message that Helen Baldwin captures in her paintings of the Aboriginal people: wisdom, simplicity, spontaneity and grace.

I met Helen Baldwin in 1986 and was captivated by the honesty and freshness of her paintings. Her technical skill is beyond question. (She studied art at East Sydney Technical College, where her teachers were Douglas Dundas, Fred Leist and Roy Davies.) My conviction that Helen's work should reach a wider audience has borne fruit with this publication. To assist me in my role as editor, Helen kindly arranged a visit to Central Australia so that I could meet some of the people and see some of the places that inspired her work. It was a profound and unforgettable experience.

Markilyi (Lizzie)

Despite her shyness and sensitivity, Helen Baldwin has an earthy humour and delights in telling stories about her journeys. This book contains many such stories. More importantly, it is a pictorial record of Central Australia and the people whose ancestors made the first footprints in this ancient land.

Laura Murray

THE COLOURS OF WILCANNIA

I have always loved exploring. With my husband Eric I have taken many trips into country and outback Australia. We took many journeys along the Barwon, Darling, Namoi and Paroo rivers in New South Wales, and arriving at the point where all these rivers meet began a new chapter in my life. At this once great meeting place for Aboriginal people, I felt a deep desire to capture its moods and colours and so initiated friendships and possibilities that have nourished twenty-five years of drawing, painting, needlework and sculpture.

We began by travelling to Wanaaring and from there along any road to anywhere. Most of these roads were barely tracks, particularly in western Queensland, and hope was often our only navigator.

Wilcannia was my first fascination: the grey soil, crazed after drought; the grey-green foliage; the creamy water of the River Darling flowing south, its banks a register of falling water levels; and the grey river gums, their dead branches blackened and as many roots showing below as there were branches above, all reflected clearly in the river.

While having a meal on our way to Broken Hill I decided that these would be the colours for my dining room chairs and fire screen. In fact, I covered almost everything in our home that could be upholstered with needlepoint – petit and gros – in the enduring colours of Wilcannia.

The Barwon River, Western New South Wales

Chair and fire screen embroidered in Wilcannia colours

The soil in this region is clay. A few drops of rain on the dirt roads were enough to make the car slip and a few drops more would bog it. We have helped many whose cars were bogged and received help ourselves in the same predicament. When it gets wet, the soil sticks to the wheels and keeps building up until they become completely clogged and won't move. At the hotel in Bourke we were allowed only a billy can of water to wash the car. At Longreach less than 5 millimetres of rain was enough to prevent us driving from the front of the house to the garage at the back.

One year we crossed the Darling at Louth, ferried over in a boat complete with lifebuoys. The water was deep, perhaps two and a half metres, and the banks sheer. A dust storm blew up just as we crossed. It was eerie, frightening: we could see no road, no living thing, only white dust. Once we were back on the road Eric took compass readings to make sure we were going in the right direction.

We recrossed the river at Tilpa where a bridge was being constructed and travelled alongside the Darling all the way to the Murray. Further south the road became a solid moving mass of tortoises! There must have been thousands, heading for the lakes to lay eggs. Many became trapped in wire netting fences en route, unable to go backwards.

On another occasion we visited White Cliffs and stayed at the one and only hotel. A pit toilet was provided complete with bag door. There was no bathroom, just muddy water from an oil drum that had to be ladled into a chipped enamel basin on a box in the courtyard in full view of all the rooms facing it. We did what we could with our ration of drinking water (one glass per room). There had been no rain that year.

After a visit to Lightning Ridge, famous for black opal, we travelled along the Barwon River towards Walgett, where we came upon a stand of enormous grey river gums. The largest one had been sawn off to make way for a power line. I lay across the stump (all 5 feet 6 inches of me – that's about 168 centimetres) with room to spare. Lying there I felt I heard the silent beating of a disappearing landscape and I became more determined than ever to paint it. I was determined, too, to paint the Aboriginal people who are so much a part of this landscape.

Seeing my paintings, a friend suggested I visit his wife's niece who lived at Haasts Bluff in the Northern Territory. From this began my friendship with Beryl and Dick Cowen at Yuendumu and with the Territory, which is still my greatest love.

Children playing, Barwon River

2

YUENDUMU

On our first trip to Yuendumu we went via Darwin. My husband Eric and I travelled out through Bourke to Barringun on the border and into Queensland. We took a shower stop in Charleville in the most stinking bore water I have ever experienced and continued through Longreach to Winton, where the town's red brick toilets were named the Ewes and the Rams. Trying to boil a billy at the Combo waterhole (the billabong which inspired 'Waltzing Matilda') proved impossible because of flies. The corks on our fly veils and large hats made no difference to them – flies got into eyes, up nostrils, into ears and, when we spoke, into our mouths.

Combo Waterhole

Such a beautiful place but ... our only alternative was to continue on our way to Tennant Creek and then to Darwin.

The trip was unbearably hot, with bush on fire everywhere. There were masses of wild geese at Newcastle Waters and an old man dried out by the sun whose ill-fitting false teeth dropped and clicked with every word he spoke. He told us that the building on the hill was the bakehouse and that the year before it had been isolated by torrential rain and great flooding. There had been water as far as one could see and food had come in by boat and helicopter. The eye can see quite a distance out there and his story seemed hardly believable. Driving from Darwin to Alice we found the country from Renner Springs was covered with flowers. It is a matter of wonderment that a drop of rain on dry earth can produce so many flowers within a few days. I had never seen such beauty: daisies of every colour, the red road stretching towards distant amethyst mountains (one flat-topped and one shaped like a cone), an aquamarine sky, here and there grey-green bushes and the grey bleached branches of dead trees. I was amazed to learn that so many of the flowers were perfumed. Surrounding Alice Springs were masses of tiny white everlasting daisies and that wonderful mulla mulla (pussytail) covering the MacDonnell Ranges in mauve and pink. Today masses of pinky red dock or wild hops seem to have taken over. These came as seeds in the stuffing of camel saddlebags brought in by the Afghans who helped open up the Centre. Harry Purvis, who flew with Kingsford Smith, took us in his small plane on our first flight over Uluru/Ayers Rock and Kata Tjuta. The small airstrip that I remember is now a thriving aerodrome, complete with tourist village.

Beryl and Dick Cowen met us in Alice Springs and took us to Yuendumu, 320 kilometres to the north-west. This is a large settlement on the edge of the Tanami Desert inhabited mainly by the Walpiri tribe. Everything was very different then. Some Aborigines had just come in from the desert to Papunya and their first contact with Europeans. There had been a terrible drought, food was very scarce, and these desert people had been on the point of starvation, keeping alive by eating the few lizards they could catch. I was entranced with Yuendumu and drove everyone crazy talking about it. This is what I would paint. From then on I was asked to stay each year with the Cowens.

Settlements in this district began as areas of land given by the government to the Aboriginal people to share in common. Previously, each tribe had its own area of land and its own language. The Luritja land was at Papunya; the Pitjantjatjarra at Uluru, Areyonga and Ernabella; the Anmatjira at Napperby and the Walpiri at Yuendumu. The Luritja language is more recent, a mixture of languages as the result of contact among different tribes. The settlement policy has proved problematic, with fights breaking out regularly, especially as alcohol has become so readily available.

My visits to Yuendumu coincided with the annual sports meeting. Aboriginal people came from near and far from all the settlements and missions to the sports, packed together in cattle trucks. The long-distance rides must have been awful; rough and hot during the day and just as cold at night, but all seemed to love it. I heard of one man who walked about 80 kilometres to ride back on one of these trucks with the girl he fancied. The oval for the sports was marked by two young boys on the back of a utility. One would let his foot hang down, his heel marking the soft earth, while the other would pour on the white marking paint, around and around, until all the lanes were completed.

The sporting events were numerous – running, jumping, softball, relays, et cetera. Only the old men competed in spear and boomerang throwing, as the young had lost the skill.

Man of Central Australia

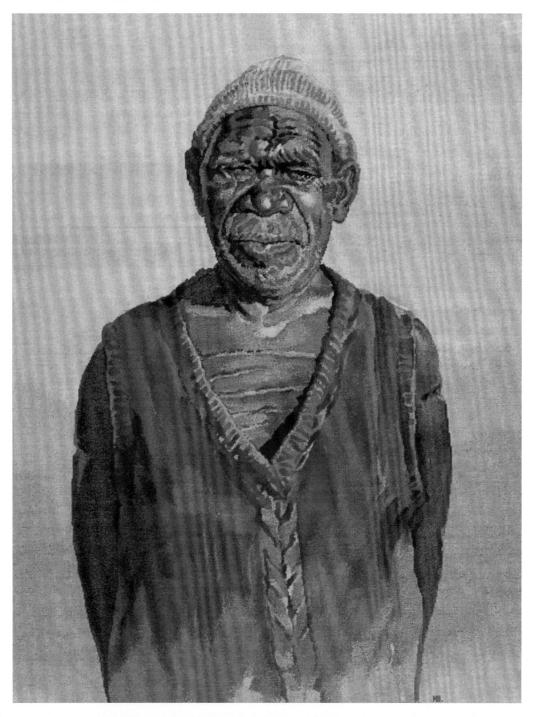

After initiation boys are considered to be men and must stay with the men; they do not run races at the sports with the boys and are called upon to do men's work. I once spoke to two youths who seemed inseparable. They just stared ahead with cold, stony faces, no emotion. The children whispered to me that girls were not allowed to speak to them as they were being prepared for initiation. The children at Yuendumu were very shy. They would sidle up behind us, gently touching our backs. If we turned they would stand and look at the ground with just the hint of a smile.

Watching the Sports, Yuendumu

All seemed as curious of us as we were of them.

Some families at Yuendumu had a concrete-brick hut, roofed, with a verandah and the ashes from a fire out the front. Mostly they sat outside the houses, which would be vacated should someone die. Child mortality was said to be high and, during one of my visits there, a Doctor of Zoology was sent to find out why. Neither the doctor nor the mothers seemed happy about this. I went with her on her rounds. She would go to each house and stand just inside the barbed wire fence. After a few minutes the mother would appear and bring out her child to be examined, and so it continued until all had been visited. Those with a problem were taken to the hospital. Yuendumu had a hospital, a supermarket and a baby health centre. Some babies were brought in by their mothers in a coolamon, carried with one arm on the hip. They were gorgeous: solemn faced with big brown eyes. The young mothers bathed and powdered them and curled their hair when they visited the centre. If there were older children, these would be carried straddle-legged on the hip, or hoisted up onto the shoulders, their legs around the mother's neck.

It did not matter if the mother was pregnant and carrying a small child; if a boy child wanted to be carried she had to carry him too.

We went hunting with three house girls north of Yuendumu, leaving details of the time we hoped to return and the direction we were taking with someone at the settlement. Tragedies occur in these vast, hot, dry areas if one is careless: too long in the sun trying to repair a broken-down vehicle or setting out to walk for help dehydrates the body and can result in death. It is much better to sit in the vehicle and wait for help.

The soil here is the most brilliant red I have seen and the country flat with odd low hills and not much vegetation. We stopped to fossick. The young women who seemed so awkward doing housework were like quicksilver in the bush. One even had a baby on each hip. In the strong sunlight their skins shone like brown satin. We climbed a small rise, and looking from the top of the rocks on this rise we saw a green, fertile

Shy child

16

Wives, Yuendumu

valley – or so it appeared – while all around it was dry and dusty. The women collected red and yellow beans from under the trees and found enormously fat witchetty grubs in the roots of bushes. Everyone returned well pleased.

One of them had left this area only once in her lifetime to go to Alice Springs. I asked her how she enjoyed it. She poured forth a mighty stream of Aboriginal words and the expression on her face made it obvious it would only be once!

3

BESWICK STATION

In the late sixties when Beryl and Dick left Yuendumu they took up residence at Beswick Station, near Katherine. The Aboriginal people here are very black with shorter arms and legs and are different in stature from the Centre folk. They are mostly small people and have had much more contact with whites.

We were privileged to see a series of dances expertly performed at Bamyili settlement, in the twilight and dust. The main dancer, Willi Martins, one of the best in the Territory, came in from the bush only for the dancing. The headman danced for us, painting himself with white and wearing a headdress of white cockatoo feathers. Two other Aboriginal men had clap sticks and a very long didgeridoo. The headman brought a chair from his home for me to sit on (I was told he was very proud of owning it), so I sat up like a queen while everyone else stood around or sat on the ground.

There was a beautiful lagoon at Beswick Station filled with waterlilies. The girls would wade in the water feeling for mussels with their feet and lift them into their skirts with their toes. Many of them, particularly the old women, smoked pipes without a stem or used crab claws as pipes. I was given some clap sticks by the headman that were hard and heavy, made of ironwood (*Acacia estrophiolata*). He belonged to the caterpillar people and had painted his story on them, the caterpillars coloured white on a background of red ochre. I sprayed

Babes in arms

them with a transparent fixative to make the paintwork hold, but the paint was rather fragile. A small didgeridoo made of ironwood and beautifully decorated by Willi Martins is lasting much better with this treatment.

A number of images stay in my mind of Beswick: like everyone scattering from an Aboriginal man who was a marvellous fencer but who went wild after a few drinks and swung his axe in all directions; or of a beautiful Aboriginal girl sitting with her children (the boy a full-blood and the baby girl at her breast a half-caste) under an applegum tree, its enormous blossoms casting a dappled light over them. The young woman kept her home spotless but preferred to sit under the gum tree with their two dogs. This made an exquisite picture which I painted on my return home and then stitched in fine petit point. It is still among my favourite works.

Barbara, Ray and Marilyn, Beswick Station

4

PAPUNYA

few years later I stayed with Geoff Lawson, a schoolteacher, and his wife Susan at Papunya. Susan came from Glenbrook as did Peter and Michael Ellis, her brothers, with whom I was to stay at various outback schools in the Territory.

Papunya was one of the most beautiful but untidy places in the Territory. Once quite heavily

Road to Mt Liebig, near Papunya

Belt Range, Papunya

populated, there has been a movement of people to outstations in recent times. The settlement
itself has altered a great deal: the mountains remain superb but red roads run in all directions like
open wounds in the bleached grass. Yet even this has changed. Where once the grass was tall and
white there are now hard tufty blobs of buffel grass seeded from the air and spreading as far west as
Mt Liebig, the highest mountain in the Territory, in the MacDonnell Ranges (80 kilometres from
Papunya). When very dry, the red dusty earth is all that the eye can see, but with rain the grass
springs up again.

Papunya is about 225 kilometres north-west of Alice Springs on a plain which stretches from Belt
Range in the south to Mt Wedge in the north. Mt Wedge is a cattle station and was once the only
source of meat for the settlement. Supplies were brought in by plane or truck but now there is a
well-stocked supermarket. When we first flew to Papunya we stopped at the Haasts Bluff settlement
before continuing around the Bluff at the eastern end of Belt Range. There is a gap in the range
and when flying back to Alice the mountains appear almost to touch the plane's wing tips. On one
such flight the pilot, being new to the area, was just as anxious as we were to see everything and

took advantage of there being no crosswind to fly low between the ranges. The rock formations were amazing. One in particular reminded me of an enormous pack of cards, some standing upright and others slipping down, their history revealed in dark markings down their sides.

Papunya Hill east of the settlement is sacred and Aboriginal women and children may not climb it. Even the schoolgirls who joined us on our walk remained at its foot. The view from the top is vast, awe-inspiring. Great plains roll before the eyes with distant odd-shaped ranges and a few very straight roads, until earth and sky become one at the horizon. The hill itself is a mass of red rocks with little vegetation other than spinifex and a few ghost gums. The largest spider web I have seen was among these rocks; the web was white and appeared to be quite thick and strong. Every few minutes of the day the colours of the mountains change from pink to mauve to brilliant blue and, one evening as the sun set and the last of its light caught the mountains, they glowed and sparkled as if painted with

Paddlers, Papunya

deep purple glitter. The MacDonnell Ranges must surely be (with the Petermanns) among the most beautiful ranges in the world.

Susan and Geoff often picnicked in the mountains, taking as many children as they could manage on the vehicle to their favourite spot – a stream dammed up for swimming! The children laughed and splashed in the cooling water and scrambled over the rocks as nimbly as wallabies. Their excitement was catching. Hungry faces would soon be upon us for biscuits and sweet milky cups of billy tea, giving energy for more boisterous activity. Searching for tucker was equally exciting and as we drove along there would be thumping on the roof and calls of 'Bush tucker!' at which we would all pour out and search amongst the tall grass and bushes for berries and fruits. Some, we were told, would cure gut ache but others would send you blind or give you gut ache if you ate too near the seed. All meat eaters, the children generally favoured kangaroo, although one girl preferred echidna.

The children were always most curious of me, particularly my long hair and the hairpins holding it up. Driving along in the car they felt my arms and sometimes, if they were brave enough, they felt my back up under my blouse or inspected my hands, feeling the backs first and then the palms, commenting in their own language to one another.

On my first visit to Papunya an imposing fellow called Nose Peg invited a friend and me to his camp. He told us that he was the head of the Pintupis and was known as Nose Peg because he had a split septum and sometimes wore a stick or bone through his nose. His camp, on the edge of the populated part of Papunya, was full of women, one old man and several children including his son and baby daughter of six weeks: He asked us to excuse him as he and his son had to go off in his truck on business. To fortify them for the journey, his wife cooked a huge piece of meat in a pot of water which the two of them ate with the greater part of two loaves of bread, topped off with well-brewed billy tea, Nose Peg drinking first from the billy and then passing it to his son. After they left I took a photograph of the old man. He asked for money – the only one on the settlement who ever did – and as I was about to hand it to him his wife jumped up, grabbed it and quickly put it in a purse that she tucked in her more than ample cleavage. One little boy then proceeded to have hysterics, rolling his bare body on the ground. No-one took the slightest bit of notice. A woman stood up, grabbed a waddy and whacked a sleeping dog on the hip. It sprang up and almost urinated on us. Our host had gone on his busy way and I suppose we were an embarrassment to them. We were upset to see some of the dogs so underfed and ill treated and yet they never leave and appear to be very faithful in guarding the camps.

Once Eric and I happened to be visiting just after a small boy had died. After lunch the wailing began. It could be heard coming from a camp a long way to the west and spread like a flame from one camp to the other until the whole area seemed to throb with the sound of great sorrow. It lasted for a couple of hours. This is usual for a child, who has been with the tribe for only a few years. With the death of an elderly person the wailing goes on for days. When someone dies every trace of that person is swept out of camp – every footprint – and the camp is set up somewhere else. If the death occurs in hospital it is swept clean. The name of the dead person must not be mentioned and anyone with the same name is renamed Kumantjayi. The ruling is very strict. We heard of the death of a boy called Steven and because his name sounded like 'seven', the schoolchildren had to miss out this number in their daily counting.

Schoolteacher Geoff Bardon was also at Papunya during this time working on behalf of the desert artists. It is largely due to his efforts that Papunya art is recognised today by the art market both in Australia and overseas. He asked me to show the artists a petit point I had done of a little girl from Beswick Station. They loved it and squeezed around me chanting 'Number 1, Number 1, good one, good one,' giving me the thumbs-up sign. I looked at their work and bought a few pieces and again they squeezed in around me until I was breathless. It only took Geoff to assure them that Mrs Helen from Sydney was a 'poor bugger' and they disappeared like magic. Bugger appeared to be a favourite word amongst them – one boy was actually named Silly Bugger.

Pintupi Camp, Papunya

5

NAPPERBY

After several years visiting Papunya, I was invited by schoolteacher Peter Ellis to stay at Napperby, a cattle station of over 5000 square kilometres in size and 225 kilometres slightly west of north from Alice Springs. Peter lived in a small fibro house just under half a kilometre from the camp of the Anmatjira tribe. A caravan close to the camp served as the school. A small plane from Alice Springs flew us out, circling before landing to give us a spectacular view of Scaly Rock, a large red

Napperby Crossing

Twenty-Mile,
Napperby

sloping rock of great crazy slabs at the base of a hill. We could see Peter run out of his house and into his truck, picking up groups of two or three children along the road, pulling up as the plane landed, with the children too shy to look at us, whispering and giggling among themselves.

Peter's mother came with me on my first visit to Napperby. We had barely arrived when we were asked if we could help cook for the school picnic up at the 'Twenty-Mile'.

The 'Twenty-Mile' was a perfect picnic spot nor' nor' east of the school. Among the rocky cliffs are large flat areas of rock and pink sand, with waterholes big enough for the children to swim in and dive from the rocks. No-one removed any clothing – it was just in and out with bodies wet and shivering in a cool breeze. The boys crowded around an old oil drum with a fire in it to grill the sausages and boil the billy for tea. The girls carried the tucker boxes from the vehicles, sharing the heavier ones while some lighter ones were carried on their heads. A few of the boys lent a hand. The loads were sometimes dropped, bundled together again and carried on. Our bread and butter was topped with rather gritty sausages and tomato sauce.

River Gums, Napperby Creek

Heating the Irons, Napperby

Walking up the creek beyond the 'Twenty-Mile' we came to a magnificent site where pure white gums grew out of a sheer red cliff stained with black water marks. The bank on the other side was orange, with white grass at the top and huge boulders of schist down in the depths that gleamed with silver mica. Among these were scattered smaller grey boulders reaching to a pool of dark water skirted by pink sand. Sunshine caught the flash of leaf and rock while Major Mitchell parrots presided in the trees close by. There was evidence of many kangaroos having been there but the area is shunned by Aborigines.

In other areas the creek is lined with magnificent red river gums leaning towards one another on either side to create an endless avenue along the pink sands.

Living Rough

Conditions in Peter's cottage were somewhat primitive but I enjoyed the isolation and surrounding beauty. There was an old combustion stove in the house which warmed the kitchen and water for two showers. The third party had to be quick on a cold morning and both nights and mornings were freezing.

One night we had an invasion of minute green insects, millions of them, all over us, in our hair, everywhere. Out came the fly spray and brooms. We swept out bucketfuls, shook our beds and got in. In the morning we swept out more bucketfuls. What a business!

Cattle and Dust

We enjoyed many picnics at Napperby where the girls made dampers to have with tea, but most of all we loved the action at the cattle yards. The dust there is a soft misty pink, not as red as the dust at Papunya and Yuendumu, and after the men have worked with the cattle it is everywhere. One sees the landscape through a haze of pink. It is especially beautiful to watch the blue smoke from the fire where the branding irons are heated curling up and wafting across the pink haze.

One year we had to get the Flying Doctor to take Peter to Alice Springs Hospital. He had a mulga splinter in his hand. These splinters are poisonous and cause a great deal of trouble. With Peter away, a companion, Winifred, and I were taken by the owner's son to the Tilmouth yards where the cattle had been brought in for branding, ear marking and castrating. On such a large property mustering is a big job. To get the cattle closer to the yards the outer bores are closed off, depriving them of water, so they come into the next bore which in turn is also closed and so on until it is possible to drive them to the yards. There is great excitement while this takes place. Some bulls had run wild in the bush for a few years and I was keen to see a particularly mean white beast called Jaws get what was coming. I didn't have the pleasure as it was impossible to get him into the next yard that day. He killed the little heifer left with him overnight and broke two of the railings.

Mustering is hard heavy work. All the men other than the manager and the owner's son were Aboriginal. The procedure is that the beasts are driven into one yard and let out one by one through another gate where they are lassoed or thrown so that they may be marked. Sometimes the animal is so strong that a rope has to be tied to the bumper bar of a truck and the truck used to pull it over. At other times up to three men pull on the rope. They loved to dress up for this work, with new shirts, hats, trousers and boots.

One lad was dressed in men's clothing far too large for him. In between breaks he would straddle the fire where the irons were heated but returned to the job without complaint when called. The year before he had been one of the older boys at the school and was getting very sure of himself. We had found two beautifully made gunyahs in the bush and rows of ashes where fires had been lit, no doubt as part of an initiation ceremony. He was probably one of the initiates.

The owner of Napperby told me he had bought three Aberdeen Angus bulls to improve the stock but at that time they weren't doing their job. I couldn't help laughing because each morning these three aristocrats strolled through Peter's yard, the largest first, an enormous beast with hundreds of kilos of beef swaying as he stalked through the yard, the other two following, smallest at rear, heads high, noses in the air, going to inspect the herd. In the meantime the white scrub bulls were busy doing their thing – they weren't so choosey!

Cattle are not the only animals to be yarded for branding at Napperby. Donkeys are brought in and castrated to reduce the numbers, and brumbies are broken in for station use. Emmanuel, one of the Aboriginal stockmen, had a great affinity with animals. His gentle 'Woo boy, woo boy' calmed even the most fearful beast. He would slip the bridle over the animal's head while flicking its legs with the reins until the time came to slide effortlessly onto its back, all the time patting it and cooing softly.

Napperby was an artist's delight, with post-and-rail fences corrugated by white ants and hung with bits of rotting hessian. Many times I visited the yards and always the wooden stock rails and windmills entranced me. At the end of the day, as the dust settled, the young fellows would ride the last steer and children would run in with great delight to throw (scruff) the calves.

Napperby Stockyards

Ding and Humbug

Peter acquired a baby dingo after lengthy negotiations at the camp. A deputation of children had knocked on the door of the cottage and said 'Clarrie has a dingo and he wants $10 for it.' Down to the camp we went to see Clarrie's dear little dingo but it soon became obvious that Clarrie didn't want to sell. Back we came then another knock – Clarrie would sell after all. So Ding was ours. That night his mournful calls assured us that he was, indeed, a dingo. (Dingoes do not bark.)

Boots (a bitch with a dash of dingo, faithful and kindly) and Lupo (a huge white and tan staghound, floppy and friendly) were put to mother him and in a few days Ding had them both under control. A trip out in the truck began with Ding under Peter's seat. At the first bump he'd yelp and each time we'd haul him out until he wandered over to lie in my lap, gently biting my hands in play before settling down to snooze.

Sunset, Napperby

Dingo Pup

Ding came in one evening at dinner time and deposited, with much delight and wagging of his tail, an absolutely stinking piece of meat with the fattest maggots I have ever seen. He was removed very promptly with a few words, and his find with him. Ding stayed with Peter for nine months. He would take him into Alice Springs and when he whistled up the dogs, Ding would come too. One night at Aningie he did not answer the whistle. Perhaps he had gone bush and found a mate. I like to think so.

Another year the star boarder was Humbug, an emu chick. He was a great trouble to me as he had to be fed on dry Uncle Toby's Oats and cooked peas. I seemed to be forever cooking dried or frozen peas. Humbug was put with the dogs for mothers at night, wrapped up beside a hot water bottle near the kitchen stove. The dogs hated Humbug, Boots most of all. I was on my own one weekend, having been assured by Peter that the chick would come when the dogs were called, but this was not to be. Humbug went bush. An old fellow came down from camp and told me that the children had retrieved him. Following his advice, I locked Humbug on the old verandah, but if I did not announce my coming with a 'Cheep! Cheep! Cheep!' he would run frantically up and down, banging his head on the walls at either end. The children teased Humbug unmercifully and I felt that I was always cleaning up after him.

Young emus look soft but are quite hard and prickly to touch. Valerie, an Aboriginal girl, warned

Boy with Emu Chick (Humbug)

Peter that no-one would be able to get near Humbug once he matured. He was already displaying the tendency to lash out with one foot if you tried to stop him with yours. Adult emus are formidable foes. We never did find out whether this was true of Humbug because he caught his head in the fence and hanged himself when he was three-quarters grown. Valerie also maintained that emu flesh is too fatty, although we saw many large pieces cooking in the campfire ashes around Napperby.

Customs

One evening just on dusk I had occasion to visit the camp. It was bustling with activity. Each home had its own fire, and quite small children were lighting grass and running around with firesticks. Women were bringing in firewood while men sat around, some with food already cooking in the ashes and others waiting in anticipation. Home was anything that made a shelter, with food kept in the fork of a tree out of reach of the many camp dogs. There was a store on the property where certain foods could be bought but bush tucker was the favourite and probably the most nutritious. Around Napperby, the red berries off the mistletoe on the mulga bushes are prized, along with the fat white witchetty grubs found in the roots of the Acacia kempeana bush. The people sit back-to-back to eat, hiding the food going into their mouths with one hand. Perhaps during times of drought food was so scarce that those eating did not want to offend. I have heard white people call one young

Gathering Berries, Napperby

girl sneaky because of her eating habits, not realising that she was following a cultural practice.

Aboriginal children have a disarming mixture of straightforward curiosity and shy innocence. They loved to look at the tin in my mouth. Their own teeth are beautiful, although now a few have fillings from eating white fellows' sugar and flour. They are very proud of these fillings. I took out my two small dentures (I wasn't proud of them) and they were fascinated as I explained how they worked. One girl couldn't bear it – she looked at me in wonder and pulled a face. Every time she saw me after that she wrinkled her nose and drew her lips back over her teeth. I felt I was a creature most horrible.

I have painted many of the children over the years. Peter kept one of Mary, a very tall lass who was fascinated by her portrait. Day after day she would arrive with a group of much smaller children who would knock on the door and chorus 'Mary wants to see herself.' Mary never asked – the other children did the asking. They would crowd in for a lengthy inspection but Mary always looked at the ground, too shy to steal a glance at her image. I doubt if she ever did but I am sure every other child from camp saw it many times.

When Aboriginal people want something they seldom ask for it themselves. It took me a long while to realise this. This custom is very little understood. A social worker I know in Katherine told me that they would like to work but cannot ask. I remember an occasion when I brought some clothing with me to give to the people at Mbunghara. One old fellow took a pair of my son's jeans which he said were 'Little bit plenty tight'. I promised I would get him a bigger pair next time I went to Alice Springs. As I sat in the truck a few days later preparing to go to Alice with Michael Ellis, the fellow appeared and asked Michael to tell me he was size seven. I could hear it all but he wouldn't tell me directly. The pants were duly purchased and delivered. Almost everyone in camp came to the school and sat with their backs to the water tank while he sat in splendour on the one and only chair in his new pants.

New Trousers, Mbunghara

6

AREYONGA

Areyonga nestles in the MacDonnell Ranges about 225 kilometres just south-west of Alice Springs. It is a smallish settlement of Pitjantjatjarra people and has a hospital, school and supermarket. The temperatures are extreme – either hot or very cold – and I found it difficult to

Mother and Child, Napperby   *Rockhole, Areyonga*

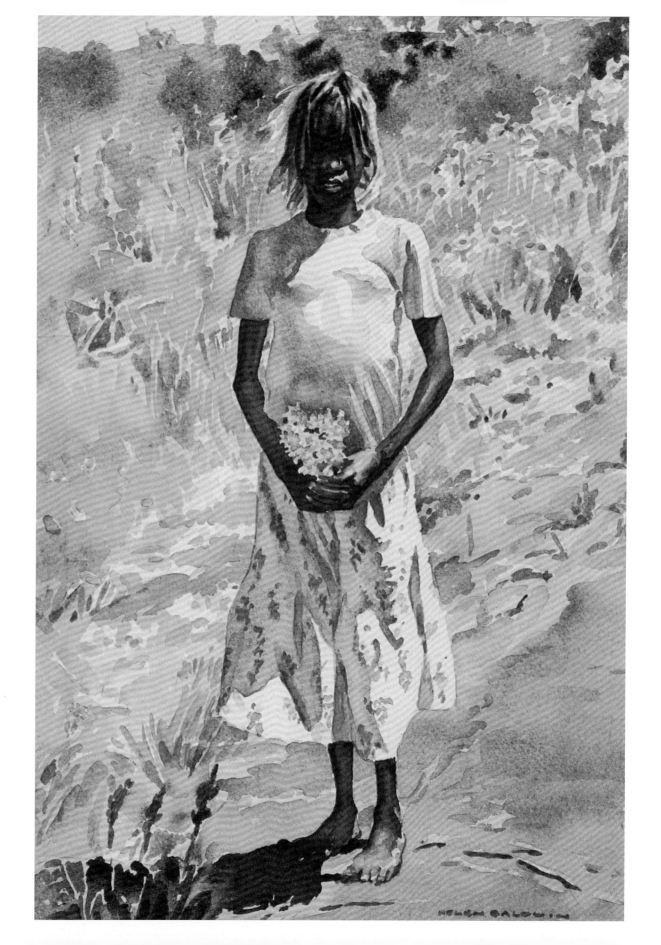

become used to the sensation that the sun here seems to rise in the west and set in the east. I visited Michael at Areyonga a number of times and enjoyed taking the children to cool off in their favourite waterhole, very deep among red rocks and towering white gum trees. Their wet chocolate-coloured bodies glistened and sparkled in the sun after a swim.

I have no Pitjantjatjarra and on our trips to the waterhole had to rely on signs and gestures to communicate, as the children are taught in their own language. I remember one little girl taking my hand and just hanging on. I could not free myself to open my bag for pencil or camera and the more I pleaded with cajoling eyes and voice the more she clung on. Even though I was desperate not to offend I eventually had to remove her hand finger by finger and free myself. I have no idea why she took such a fancy to me. Before we left for home she shyly presented me with a posy of bush flowers that she had gathered.

There are many wild flowers of different varieties at Areyonga – mint bushes, wild passionfruit, mulla mulla, yellow daisies and many more. There were expeditions with the women and children to look for wild onions – small, round, nutty flavoured delicacies that they dig for in groups for hours on end, filling up their tins to take back home. Everyone here chews pituri, a little green ball that rests on the bottom lip and is popped into the mouth as desired. It has a narcotic affect. Pituri is made from the wild tobacco leaf and mixed with white ash from ghost gum twigs.

Once a week the elders would gather and sit in a circle to discuss the affairs of the settlement. They are proud, erect men who wear distinctive red headbands as a mark of their authority within the tribe.

Each morning the pastor rang what sounded like a cow bell to call the people to prayer. It was bizarre to see them wrapped in their blankets staggering to the sermon. This was given in the Arunta language, not in their own Pitjantjatjarra, and sometimes fights would break out. In fact, the settlement was dogged by drinking and gambling, with all-night sessions sometimes when the children would talk excitedly about 'big money' and the darkness would be torn by shouts and screams. Men and women drank red wine like water, as if it was their last drink for a long time. Morning would find an aftermath of bitterness, with the people complaining and abusive – I saw one woman lift a tarpaulin off the roof of a humpy and toss it with ease into the gully. Another dragged her relations to a neighbouring camp, all of them protesting about who knows what. On my second visit I took out a watercolour portrait of Tjala, an Aboriginal assistant at the school, which he asked to buy. I asked the teacher to give it to him and was later told he was delighted with it. It seems he had just taken a young wife and had dyed his greying hair black. I did other portraits – one specifically requested by Neil Bell, a former principal at Areyonga – of Renee, a young girl who used to care for his children. Renee was so pleased with being painted that for one week twice each day she came to the house just to smile shyly at me. Soon I had more requests than I could deal

Mareeta's Posy

with, especially from the men. (This is unusual because in other places when I had asked to paint the men they had refused with a definite 'No, Missus'.) As soon as I reached for my camera, however, out would come the combs and the naturalness would be ruined. I tried to dissuade them, but to no avail.

On one occasion there was great excitement at the school because a team of fossil geologists from Adelaide University were visiting the abandoned azurite mine a few kilometres out of Areyonga. Everyone piled onto the utility, teachers and children all agog with anticipation. When we arrived there we were shown a fossil so minute that we had to view it through a magnifying glass! A gastropod, we were told, proving that this area had once been an inland sea. The children's faces showed outraged bewilderment and, as Michael said, 'It had a disgusting name anyway.'

Some years after my first visit to Areyonga I stayed with a linguist there and was surprised by the way the settlement had altered for the better. Busloads of tourists came in once a week and a room was desperately needed for the display and sale of artefacts. I helped out with the project. Meanwhile the 'Artefacts Department' sat in the shade of a few trees, the men carving boomerangs, clap sticks and so on and the women decorating them with an iron heated in the fire, much like poker work. The women were being encouraged to do batik work and a Pitjantjatjarra news bulletin was being printed for them in their own language. They told their stories to a linguist who translated them into Pitjantjatjarra. The artist Thomas illustrated the stories that his mother had told him and made a book.

Inyika, Areyonga

7

MBUNGHARA

When Peter married he left Napperby and went to teach at Yirara College in Alice Springs. Peter's parents and Eric and I chartered a small plane and flew out for the wedding via Charleville and Bidouri to Alice. The flight took us over some of the driest country in the continent, known as the Channel Country, watered only by rivers during occasional floods. Viewed from the air the rivers spread like dark arteries over a bare land of superb earthy colours. Before the wedding we stayed at Napperby with Peter and then drove to meet his brother halfway between there and Mbunghara. Michael, who was now teaching at Mbunghara, took us the rest of the way. It was our first visit to Mbunghara and the evening drive was filled with the colour and perfume of wild

Mt Ziel to the South

West to Mbunghara

tobacco plants blooming beside the road. The red earth, the fragrance and the grey blue-green of the vegetation were magical and, to me, another touch of the Dreaming.

Much of the country around the Mbunghara area was taken up by Narwietooma, a cattle station of 2600 square kilometres situated about 225 kilometres just north-west of Alice Springs. It belonged to the late Eddie Connellan who had owned the small bread-and-butter planes that once flew to far-flung settlements and stations. They provided a wonderful service around the country. Many times my husband Eric and I sat patiently at Alice Springs aerodrome hoping we could get on. Neither of us is small and the plane could carry only a certain weight but we always seemed to manage it.

An area of about 1 hectare was set aside for a school for the Luritja people who had always lived at the foot of Mt Ziel. They numbered about thirty and soon became used to my annual visits. Michael lived in a large caravan close by the portable schoolhouse and ablution block. On my first visit the Aboriginal camp was situated west of the school. I am sure the Aboriginal people prefer homes of their own making. They always choose a site in the centre of a flat area with a clear view all around as mamu (ghosts) are ever present after dark. The people had been anxious to make sure of their own piece of land and had very carefuly fenced it all in. Then someone died so they moved out of the fenced area nearer to Dashwood Creek, with Mt Ziel to the south-east and Mt Heughlin to the west. The land here is covered with what the children called punti bushes. In spring these are resplendent with yellow flowers and the ground around them is carpeted with yellow and white daisies and round mulla mulla bushes.

Peppercorn trees line the road leading to the dam. Many are broken by the cattle as they come for water; the bulls especially trample any young tree or bush in their path. The brumbies arrive at dusk – manes and tails flying – a stallion with his brood, the foals galloping alongside their mothers. The drumming of hooves at nightfall signals their return to the bush.

Sunsets at Mbunghara are magnificent. The entire western sky, so expansive out here, glows orange-red behind the silhouetted trees. At dawn the same brilliant sky is fired by the huge yellow ball of the sun. Butcherbirds call, the camp stirs, little night animals go underground and suddenly, after a cold night, everything is ready for another hot day.

Children and Bush Picnics

There were many picnics among the foothills of Mt Ziel and in special places along Dashwood Creek. In one spot the creek has cut through a huge, brilliantly red sandhill known as Mali Pata. Here the children love to climb the 9-metre bank on one side and slide down again. On the other side of the creek the sand ends as the bush begins. Picnics always included damper and tea. Once Michael's mother made toffee that we broke into pieces and handed around. Later the children came running up asking for more broken bottle! The dry creek bed is dotted with majestic river red gums (*Eucalyptus camaldulensis*), whose light grey bark peels to leave splendid white trunks. The children delighted in one particularly enormous tree with many trunks and great spreading branches. They called it itara. The leaves of the gum trees are abundantly frosted with prultji (pronounced

prutja by the children), a white sugar-encrusted insect that has a sweet eucalyptus flavour and is very good tucker. The children would gather branches and sit picking off this delicacy, munching away and then collecting some in enamel school mugs for later. One boy took off his jeans, tied the legs together and filled them with prultji to take back to camp. Arkatjiri is another favourite, a small,

Sunset, Mbunghara

dried-up berry with a very strong flavour that can be picked from the underside of low bushes. The search for tucker – and the eating – was constant. Every now and then the children would climb the gums for more, bringing back little birds' nests complete with eggs for us to see. They were made to put them back but nothing seemed to dampen their enthusiasm. More nests kept coming.

It was very difficult to do anything but quick sketches on these occasions because as soon as the children saw pad and pen you were surrounded. One boy pointed to a sketch of himself and said 'Me?' I nodded and soon he had the entire book in pieces, picking out all his friends with great excitement. Pages had to be collected from near and far after this episode.

We had picnics to Ungkungku on Glen Helen Station where the children climbed the red rocks and swam. That altered with new owners. On one occasion a woman had to be taken to Papunya Hospital with a bad ankle. The drive there was magnificent, through mountains that seemed to go on and on in ever increasing beauty. Whenever the utility went to Papunya it was loaded with relatives of a sick person and would be piled high with bedding or other possessions. It is unbelievable just how many can fit into such a limited space.

The First Footprints, Dashwood Creek

Alison's Mug of Prultji, Dashwood Creek

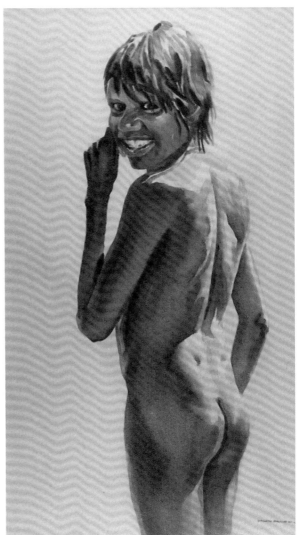

Henry, Mbunghara

The people are great trackers. One evening after dark word came from camp that a hunting party was late returning. Eric, Michael and two children set out to look for them using only a torch and the headlights of their vehicle. Justin, a young schoolboy, tracked them through the bush for about 30 kilometres and found the group gathered happily around a fire. They clambered aboard and the overloaded vehicle was driven back to camp.

Michael built a small canteen at Mbunghara to give the people access to fresh fruit and other foods necessary for their good health but the old people had no idea of coming before or after school so there were constant interruptions to the teaching and the canteen had to be stopped.

The schoolroom was filled with children from any age to early teens and the dress was unpredictable. One young girl wore a thick topcoat for days on end despite the unbearable heat. Others appeared in long skirts and tops that tumbled from their shoulders, yet their natural grace is such that they always managed to climb trees, play games like hockey and baseball, and look elegant. The little boys seldom wore anything. It was such a sight to see them working hard at their desks, producing such clean, tidy work. One boy, when he was fed up, would get to his feet and yell 'Ick of it, ick of it!' Another girl would react by lying face down outside the school, moaning and kicking her feet. It never lasted long, however, and she would come back to the classroom and settle down to work.

My long hair was another cause of interruption to the school day. As I stood in the sun to dry it the school caravan would tilt as the children crowded to the windows to take a look. Once I wore my hair down while in the caravan and all except one child (who kept trying to brush it away from my face) insisted on feeling it. The babies were another matter – they couldn't bear the sight of me. One couple sought help with their infant who had an ulcerated mouth. I had to sit in the bathroom and call out what I thought, because whenever I put my head around the corner the

Canteen, Mbunghara   *Young Man, Mbunghara*

screaming began! Mothers got very concerned when their children were ill although they did not appear to do much about it. Even adults walked off and offered no help to each other. I have given a shoulder to assist someone to the car for Michael to drive them to hospital or back to camp. Once in hospital, however, the relations are very attentive and sit on the floor beside the patient until he or she recovers.

Tribal laws were still strict in the outback. Skin names are a very important part of tribal life – most tribes have eight different skin names, although the Gibson Desert people have only four. These names show the relationship of the people with one another. It is taboo for certain skins to marry, thus ensuring the purity of the race. A couple who married at Mbunghara were banished from camp because their skin relationship was wrong. The young woman paid a visit to Mbunghara while the men were away to show off her baby girl, but that was the last I heard of her. The women generally go to hospital now to have their babies; in former times they went into the bush accompanied by an aunt. The aunt would massage the woman from behind, deliver the baby and cut the cord with her strong nails. The newborn baby would then be blanketed with earth or bark. Twins seldom survived. Even then there were only a few and never on the same settlement. No woman in a tribal situation could have managed with two babies, such was the harshness of the land and the way of life it imposed.

That's Entertainment

During the years that I visited Mbunghara a couple of bushies, Rex and Alan, were frequent callers. They were uncle and nephew and worked on Narwietoorna Station. I don't think they ever removed their hats. We decided to pay them a call one Sunday, their day of rest from their work at No. 8 Bore. They lived in a long caravan which had a bunk at each end and a table completely covered in beer cans. A clothes line was stretched between the caravan and a dumpty (as the toilet was colloquially known), and washing was blowing merrily in the breeze. Rex's mother lived at St Marys, New South Wales – he didn't get home too often. When I suggested that I telephone her on my return to Sydney he was delighted and told me to tell her he was full of grog and disease. I did so and she laughed excitedly. 'That's Rex,' she said, 'that's Rex!' He visited Lightning Ridge for his holidays – a suburb of Sydney as far as he was concerned. The real outback was Narwietoorna.

Not all the Aborigines like to drink. One old man from Mbunghara who did his best to keep drink off the settlement drove a group of women into Alice Springs. When he pulled up for a comfort stop on the way home, he was horrified to see the girls enjoying a carton of beer on the back of his truck.

One day after school there was great excitement when bees swarmed on a bush near the dam. There were cries of 'Honey bee, honey bee' and sticks and catapults appeared out of nowhere.

Schoolboy, Mbunghara

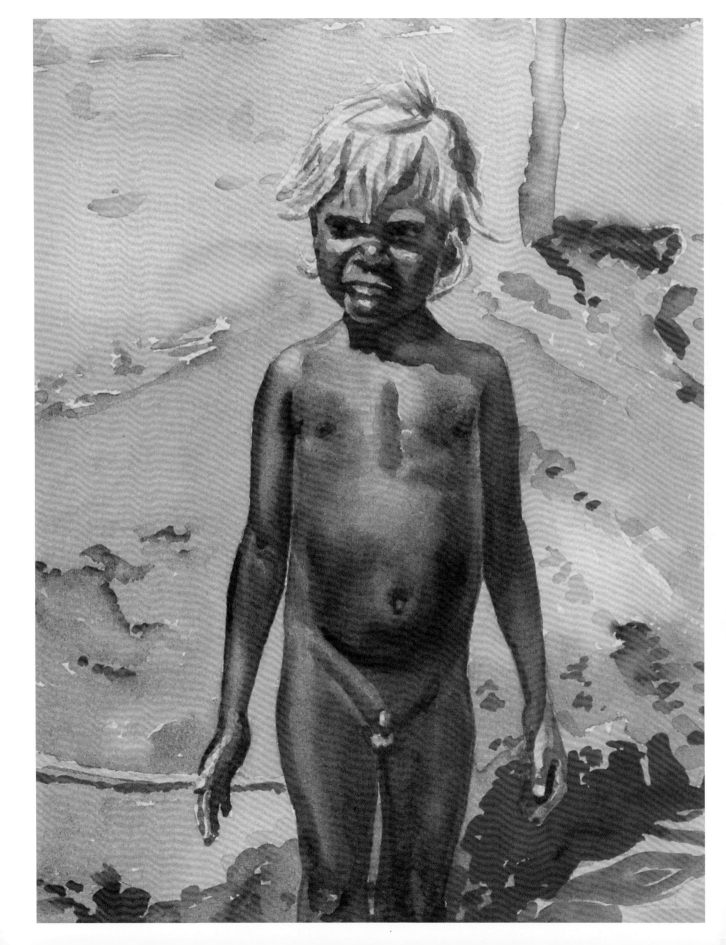

Everyone was stung a few times, only to be operated on by a girl with a rusty safety pin. There were no complaints: scars and stings are considered honorable decorations.

Once a week we had a disco at the school – the children loved it. We all joined in, the boys dancing together and the girls dancing together. They were asked to draw the disco in class after one memorable night and I was presented with the best drawing. It was by Gabrielle Possum. (Both Gabrielle and her father Clifford Possum are now well known in the art world.) There I was in my slacks, the largest figure by far in every drawing. There were film nights too, which the people loved. They crowded in and those without chairs sat on the ground. A few dogs would sneak in and dog fights sometimes broke out. I enjoyed the audience but couldn't bear the films – all cops and robbers and noise and fighting. Michael was kept busy attending to the electric generator as well as the projector. The people were very sad when they heard Michael was to leave Mbunghara, to teach at Yirara College in Alice Springs as his brother Peter had done. 'Who will look after us?' they kept asking. After he had left an old blind man sent word that the people wanted to give him a party. They took him to a beautiful spot along Dashwood Creek where they ate and drank and there was much talk.

Gabrielle Possum, Mbunghara

8

CHAMBERS PILLAR

In 1982 Michael Ellis married Lizzie (Markilyi), a full-blood Aboriginal girl from Docker River, a settlement in the Petermann Ranges on the edge of the Gibson Desert in the Northern Territory's south-western corner. Her mother and father belong to the Ngaanatjarra tribe. Lizzie is a beautiful, very capable and generous person who has made it possible for me to see places that would be inaccessible or off-limits to most travellers.

It was the year of their marriage that I first experienced kangaroo cooked in the Aboriginal way. A friend from Papunya had caught and prepared it the night before and we drove out of Alice Springs along the South Road to find a suitable place for feasting. This achieved, we were instructed to dig a large hole in the sand and make a fire in it. We held the kangaroo over the flames to singe off the fur and, when the fire had died down to ashes, placed it in the hole with potatoes and onions and covered it all with hot sand. During the long wait for our meal we all wandered off to do our own thing. I sketched and photographed, enjoying the solitude.

I'll never forget how good that meal tasted – succulent meat and vegetables, followed by damper with lashings of Peter's homemade orange jam and a large mug of billy tea.

The highlight of this visit was my trip to Chambers Pillar (Itirkawara), a large monolith 320 kilometres south of Alice Springs, on the edge of the Simpson

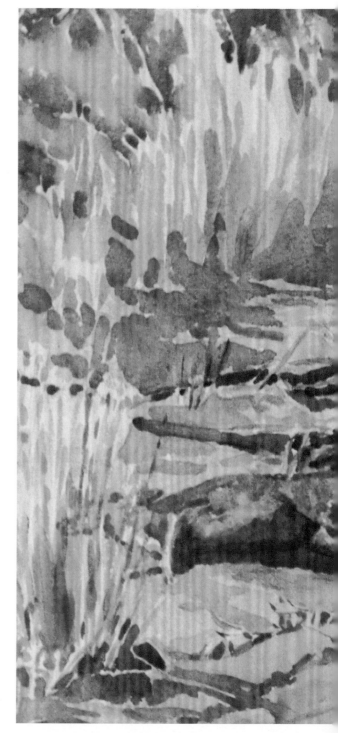

Cooking Kangaroo

56

Desert. The Pillar rises 30 metres above a 15 metre plinth and is the remains of a tabletop mountain worn away by an ancient inland sea. It was discovered by John McDouall Stuart in 1860 and named after a friend who financed his expedition across the continent.

Itirkawara is within an area declared as national park on the Idracowra Cattle Station. It was once a place of great significance for the Arantja tribe. However, continuous dust storms from

surrounding cattle stations eventually silted up the waterhole and they could no longer live there.

The Pillar is called Itirkawara after a legendary gecko ancestor of the Arantja people. A brave and bold warrior of the Arantja tribe, Itirkawara made his way to Queensland doing wonderful deeds but broke the law by having marriage relations with girls related to his mother-in-law. He even brought one of the girls back to his own camp as a wife, for which he was turned to stone. The rock just over a kilometre from the Pillar is the girl, who turned her face away in shame as the curse took effect.

Lizzie and the children dug for yams, long fleshy bulbs about 5 centimetres long, in the red earth surrounding the Pillar. They had to take care among the spinifex, whose blooms belie the cruel spikes of the grey-green bush beneath. As the purple shadows of evening threw long ribbons across the vast dry land, Lizzie became anxious about mamu, (bad spirits of the night), and I was inclined to believe her. How different, to see this eerie landscape transformed by rain four years later into endless perfumed carpets of yellow and white flowers.

While having lunch in a sheltered place between some mountains not far from Deep Well, an Aboriginal girl of the Ngaanatjarra tribe showed me an ant-lion's nest along the roadside, a conical sandpit with a hole in the centre. Placing her forefinger in the hole she brought out a tiny grey-green creature like a miniature porcupine. She explained that the young girls of her tribe place them on their breasts and nipples to bite them and make them large. She said that it hurts. Her breasts were beautiful, with nipples like large ripe mulberries. I asked about the round scars on her legs and arms and she told me that when a tribal girl becomes a woman she burns these marks somewhere on her body. This girl had four marks on the inside and outside of her legs above the ankle and on her arms above the wrist. Most seem to have them there, although her mother had marks across her chest, which must have been very painful. The process is simple: a piece of wood is taken from a bush, made red hot in a fire and applied to a wet spot on the flesh until it burns out. Inflicting pain on oneself without complaint is very much admired and a sign of great courage.

Girls from the Ngaanatjarra tribe decorate their hair with nuts from eucalyptus trees. A hair is placed in the end of a green nut, the sap of which sticks to it like glue. This is repeated until the face is surrounded by tiny nuts. One girl remembered her grandmother having hair to the waist. The nuts she had placed there in her youth still remained.

After lunch we drove to the Hugh River, which begins in the Mt Gillen Range and flows to the Finke. Here the white trunks of the gums shone in the evening light against the dry pink sand of the river bed. The only marks to disturb the surface were the tracks of a vehicle that had swerved out from the crossing and back again. The drive through Maryvale to Chambers Pillar was extremely rough. We arrived just as the sun dipped, bathing Itirkawara in vivid red light. Others had set up camp before us and we felt quite irked by their presence, unreasonably so but we felt the country to be ours.

Markilyi (Lizzie)

58

Waterhole, Hugh River

That night we saw the red eyes of a fox in the darkness as we sat around our fire. Morning revealed his tracks around our camp. I had awakened before dawn to an icy grey stillness. As I watched, the sky in the east lightened and in an instant everything was fired by the brilliance of the desert sun; the Pillar glowed a deep red and camel tracks shone like magical belts around the sandhills. Another day had begun.

9
DOCKER RIVER

My first trip to Docker River was in 1983. To prepare me for the rigours of camping we took an overnight trip to Mt Ooraminna, about 130 kilometres south of Alice. Uru minna means large water and refers to permanent water in the rockhole on top of the mountain. We drove there via the old South Road, turning left towards the distant purple mountains, and set up camp in a creek bed. Curry was heated in an old iron pot over the fire. Sleep came easily that night, although I remember being cautioned by Lizzie not to look at the stars. A man once looked at the stars from a creek bed and was washed away in a flash flood.

We followed a breakfast of bacon, eggs, toast and tea with a good deal of lying about. By midday it was quite hot so Lizzie constructed a shelter for us from branches and a blanket. Late in the afternoon we joined the road from Santa Teresa, an old Spanish mission, driving through

Mt Ooraminna

Mountain Pass, Ooraminna

orange-coloured rocky mountains flecked with white, like sugar crystals on a cake. At one place there appeared to be a series of stone walls running parallel to one another, looking far more man-made than natural. We stopped to boil a billy in another very red, very dry creek bed shaded by large coolabah trees, one in particular extremely beautiful with its grey bark and grey-green foliage lying aslant the bank. Flies were the only problem but when I complained Lizzie simply rearranged some sticks in the fire, resting their ends on a small mound of sand and, within moments, they disappeared.

We resumed our driving and from then on the flowers were superb – mulla mulla of the round bushy type and daisies, daisies, daisies, like a heavy fall of snow. In fact, they are often called desert snow daisies. The spinifex on the hills was also in flower and as the breeze caught it the whole mountain appeared to sway. It was evening when we reached Alice Springs.

Within a few days we were on the road again, this time to Docker River, taking a break at the Finke River for urgent repairs to the air conditioner. We numbered five adults, three small children and three dogs, and the heat was stifling. I spent the night at Erldunda Motel and the others camped, a good decision of mine since it turned windy during the night and they had to move camp twice. The next day we travelled west beyond the Kata Tjuta National Park boundary and lunched under our favourite desert oaks (*Casuarina decaisneana*). The young ones remind me of little hairy men, quite different from the adult trees with their long, pendulous foliage.

Lasseter's Cave in the hill beside a creek bed prompted a decision to stop and explore. A few old people at Docker River still remember Lasseter. They took food to the cave but he suspected it was poisoned and asked instead to be taken to a creek where he later died. Whilst we were looking about near the cave a curious fellow with a beard peered in and left. Meeting up again at the vehicle we burst out in unison 'I think I saw Lasseter!' and then shrieked with laughter at ourselves.

That night we camped at Hull Creek where you can wander in shoulder-high grass without fear of prickles, a rare treat in the desert. On our left were Giles Fallen Ramparts, part of the Petermanns and so called by the explorer of the same name. In the distance to our left was Blood Range.

Snow Daisies, Ooraminna

One mountain in the range at Docker River stands alone, a sacred mountain of deepest amethyst that only the men are allowed to climb.

Sister Pat welcomed us at Docker River with tea and chocolate cake. A nursing sister from Windsor in England, she lived alone in this remote corner of Australia, loved and respected by the Aboriginal people under her care.

Feeling refreshed, we continued our drive across Docker River and into the hills. The grass beside the road was thick and golden, disturbed only by a few rabbits or the odd camel. Prickly wattle (*Acacia victoriae*) was in bloom, great stretches of intense yellow blossoms among dark green foliage against a backdrop of mauve mountains. The sun shone brilliantly on all this and the red tracks along which we travelled to Tjilpuka Rockhole – one of the few with permanent water – were shaded by majestic white eucalypts growing out of pink sand at the water's edge. The rocks appeared dark in the shadows but the feeling was golden.

After a swim we boiled the billy and had lunch, returning to Docker River and the main road to Alice Springs about mid-afternoon. En route we pulled out a car that had become bogged in the sand. It belonged to two Aboriginal men who continued on their way to Blood Range undaunted, off the road and into the bush. It was obvious they would never make it in that vehicle. We planned to camp at our favourite spot under the desert oaks but someone was there before us. Furious, we drove closer to Kata Tjuta and found an even better spot (although the grumbling kept on) where we ate well and fell asleep to the sighing of the oaks and the gentle rattle of the pods on the creamy desert grevilleas (*Grevillea stenobotrya*).

Desert Oaks   Sister Pat

Prickly Wattle, Petermann Ranges

Morning found us agreeing that it was the nicest spot anyone had ever camped in and the other lot of the night before didn't know what they had missed! Kata Tjuta looked magnificent in the strengthening sun, casting purple shadows across a sea of golden grass. It was hard to leave them and continue the journey home.

Tucker and Stories

The following year found me again at Docker River, this time just with Michael, Lizzie and their daughter, Lucy. Lizzie was pregnant again and keen to see her family. I met Mr and Mrs Giles, Lucy's tjamu and kabahli (grandfather and grandmother) and sat with them in their camp. As we boiled a billy I was told that they drink bore water here and have to walk a fair distance to a tap for it. Later we went digging for witchetty grubs (maku) with the women in Lizzie's family. I learnt later that in their tribe only one man may go with the women so, naturally, Michael was the one man.

We drove along the road to the Western Australian border, across a plain where grass trees grow among the spinifex and mulga. I expressed an interest in them and Lizzie was asked by her mother to tell their story. She interrupted now and then to make corrections or add details in her own Ngaanatjarra language.

Lizzie began by pointing out a mountain on our left with a line of trees running down its side. These were the warriors of the tribe coming to punish a man from the mountain to our right who had taken one of the women of the tribe. He was a bad man and treated her cruelly. They came across to his mountain and speared him in the gut. As he was dying he vomited out across the plain and where he spat the grass trees grew.

Rockhole at Tjilpuka

As we drove off the road in among sandhills, grass and mulga, I was preoccupied with thinking about how to mix the colours of this landscape on my palette. They look simple but are subtle and difficult to achieve. They also vary from minute to minute. What hope is there to catch such beauty on a piece of paper with a brush and paint?

I was brought back to the present by Michael's announcement that we had a puncture, so it was all out for maku while he made the repairs. A long steel rod, like a mini crowbar, is used to dig for

Tjamu and Yuntjin (Lucy with her grandfather)

Grass Trees near the Border of Western Australia, Petermann Ranges

maku which are found in the roots of bushes. The grubs later emerge as moths. They are delicious eaten either raw or lightly cooked in the fire and are rich in protein and fat. The women become absolutely absorbed in their task and on this occasion seemed to be going farther and farther into the bush to find the right bushes. I was afraid I might not be able to make it back so decided to return to the car, calling out that if I were not there before them I would be on the sand ridge. The bushes were not thick and it did not seem a hard thing to do but after much walking I still could not see the car. I walked up and down the sandhill and got close enough to hear Michael's tapping but it took ages to find him. It is very easy to get lost.

We drove back at that special time of day when the shadows are long and you feel at one with nature, part of it all. There is nowhere else like it and if you haven't been there you could not understand. It is somehow part of the Dreaming, eternal, beautiful, the sacred mountain and its magical colour so serene.

Looking for Maku, Petermann Ranges

The next day we set out earlier and drove across the Docker River into the mountains on the right. We began climbing and eventually came to an enormous plateau of white grass where a large camel ran in front of us – hump, rump and tail flop-flopping and mouth frothing. The vehicle rocked with laughter. As Lizzie said, her people love to laugh and so do I. Maybe that's why we get along so well.

We crossed the plateau to its border of grey-green mulga. This was where the honey ants would be found. The women choose a likely bush where they see small ant holes and scrape away the surface earth. When they find a few more ant holes together they begin to dig with their steel rods and very soon have dug themselves into an enormous hole. It looks like a rabbit warren, every now and then revealing ants clinging in a cluster to the ceiling like a bunch of grapes, honey-coloured and clear where the sun catches them. Lizzie showed us how to prepare some flattish bark to put them on, shaped like a coolamon and lined with soft earth in the old way so that the ants would remain intact. The ant itself is the size of a tiny black domestic ant, with an abdomen as big as a garden pea. Worker ants collect nectar and inject it into the soft abdomens of the storer ants, which hang upside down on the roof in clusters. In hard times they regurgitate the honey and sustain the colony. To eat them you hold the head and bite off the honey sack. It is more liquid than ordinary honey but similar in flavour and varies slightly from nest to nest according to the nectar collected.

One of the women found and killed a rabbit. I did not see it gutted, but for cooking the fur was singed in the fire and the carcass put in the ashes legs up. We all sat around waiting patiently for it to cook. Another of the women handed us each a portion. Normally I loathe rabbit but this animal was delicious, perhaps because of the cooking or the grasses on which it lived.

We drove west coming back. The sky was spectacular, a vast mass of dark swirling clouds with the golden sunset behind them. I commented that surely these were rain clouds but I was told it was only wind behind them. We passed an outcrop of slate, white and dark red in the evening light with a few grey-green corkwood trees and, of course, the grass. Suddenly someone saw a rabbit so Michael was on the back of the vehicle with his rifle. Lizzie took over the wheel. In all we collected seven rabbits and pulled up a bit further on to do the gutting ready for the hungry mouths back at camp. The women first cracked the joints (to make it easy to break the carcass into pieces and hand around when cooked) and a small hole was made with a knife or sharp stone on the lower right-hand side of the abdomen. A finger went in, drew out the bottom part, in again and the top half came out, leaving only heart and liver behind. The fur was plucked and placed in the cut to stop sand getting in and then all were dumped in the back and the journey resumed.

Morning found us driving to Kintore along the road to Western Australia, taking a couple of turns along the way and heading north. We called at the Pankupirri Rockhole where there were quandong trees covered in bright red fruit (not yet ready to eat) and a couple of wild plum trees. The plums were the size of currants. There were many sandhills, low shrubs and beautiful grass. It was the edge of the Gibson Desert and camels were a common sight. We made camp while it was still light somewhere over the Western Australian border. This time a tent was erected for me and Lizzie made a shelter of bushes at the head of their swag. It had ice on it the next morning.

Rabbiting

Wind behind Clouds,
Petermann Ranges

10

KINTORE

Kintore is a plains settlement with abundant white grass and a small mountain range dominated by Mt Leisler. The people at Kintore moved from Papunya to be on their own much as the Pintupis had done when they moved to Yai Yai, sister to Papunya, fifteen or so years earlier. I was at Yai Yai when everyone was making gunyahs or some sort of shelter so that they could live in the Pintupi tribal manner but as time went by they wanted a hospital and schooling for the children. A great deal of money was spent and now it has ceased to exist. Kintore, however, is still thriving.

Some years ago five Gibson Desert Aborigines arrived at an outpost of Kintore for marriage reasons. None had seen white people before. Their relations gave them clothes and food. The desert people had

Lucy

Papunya Range

great dignity and pride and found the way of life at Kintore difficult. One man returned to the desert on his own.

Lizzie had relations at Kintore and wanted to show them her new daughter. She sat with the women in a circle on the ground. I would love to have joined them but thought as it was my first visit it would be taking a liberty. Later Lizzie told me to join in whenever I pleased. They all gave a gift of money for Lucy, whose Aboriginal name is Yuntjin, after one of her grandmothers. When a child is christened there is a ceremony – something like laying on of hands – and chanting to wish the child well. To ensure the baby will have beautiful hair, a single strand is taken from a good head

of hair and placed upon the baby's head.

At Kintore the men wear red headbands and walk with a dignity that is fast disappearing. We refuelled and I met one of Lizzie's uncles before setting off for Papunya. Lizzie took the opportunity to dig for maku during a lunch stop. The area was delightful, red sandhills covered in spinifex, masses of pale pink mulla mulla among the grey-green bushes and a few desert oaks. The day was warm and overcast and soon found us back on a wide new highway that goes somewhere kilometres to the west. Mt Liebig came into view, veiled in distant shades of burnt sienna, amethyst and deepest purple. What appears to be one mountain becomes many as the light alters or the clouds throw their shadows across the land.

We arrived at Papunya and stayed overnight with friends of Michael. The others camped outside the house (there were other visitors) and I had my swag on the study floor between schoolbooks, Aboriginal artefacts, paintings and a bowl of goldfish. Alistair, also a teacher, and his Aboriginal wife Ada were most hospitable and we were assured of a hot shower and breakfast.

The next day we arrived back in Alice Springs, after a trip of over 2000 kilometres. We rested for a day or two and then became swept up in the tenth anniversary celebrations at Yirara College.

Yirara College was begun by David Odling-Smee, an Englishman whom I met at the celebrations. He had a great love of the Aboriginal people and knew all the skin names of his students and their families, which is very important to them. It is a very lonely time when the children come in to college as not all of them speak the same language. There are some European advantages but it must be cold comfort for a young person leaving camp-living and a culture that they love. The four walls must drive them crazy after the bush and its vastness. Many run away and who can blame them?

Women from Amata, Dancing, Yirara College Fete 1984

11

RETURN TO DOCKER RIVER

My next visit to Docker River was in 1985 with Michael, Lizzie, Lucy and baby Emma (Nutji Nutji). This time we travelled via Wallara Ranch, Kings Canyon and the main road to Uluru.

We rolled out swags and lit a fire at Curtin Springs, close to Mt Ebenezer, relaxing with our evening meal in the fresh air and silence. Morning found us untroubled by ghostly mamu, contrary to Lizzie's fears, and ready for a substantial breakfast. Lucy had been for a walk in the bush with her mother and wanted to go back again to see or get some particular thing. Lucy by this time was almost three years old. Lizzie bent down, touched Lucy's foot and said 'Lucy's tjina' then pressed the foot into the soft soil and pointed to the footprint. 'See Lucy's tjina? Now follow Lucy's tjina.' The child nodded and did just that.

On the road again, Yulara Village provided a shower stop before passing Uluru and Kata Tjuta on our way through the National Park to the desert oaks. Here Lizzie collected some maku and strung them onto a grass thread. No doubt this is how the grubs were carried before the advent of tins or mugs.

After half an hour's drive we came upon a broken-down car belonging to some Pitjantjatjarra people, three women, one man and six small boys from Areyonga. We stopped to help. Apparently the men had seen an old car further back that had the parts needed to repair the vehicle and had gone to get them.

Soon a roadside fire was going and we were handing around tea and mandarins, which the little boys loved. The children were in their element, running here, there and everywhere, crawling in and out of bushes, their bare bodies so right against the colours of the earth. One of the women nursed a sleeping baby on her lap while the other two women called each of the little boys to help fetch wood for the fire. On the horizon where the red dusty road ended the hazy mauve silhouette of Kata Tjuta shimmered in the sun. There was so much here to sketch and paint.

Lucy with maku on grass thread

Markilyi, Yuntjin and Nutji Nutji (Lizzie, Lucy and Emma)

Tea was soon over and the ashes nearly out when suddenly the bush was alight. The boys had set fire to the dry spinifex with their lighted sticks. Within seconds the women were up off the ground, over the bank and the fire was out. I was amazed by their speed. Not long after the men returned, the car was fixed and we resumed our separate ways.

Friends had helped me collect clothes and beanies to take out as gifts for Lizzie's relations. This is not necessary but I like to repay her people for their kindness in taking me to so many special places. Mr Giles shook my hand and said 'You come again.' They were all delighted with the clothes, especially the beanies, which from then on were never off their heads. Mr Giles asked Michael where I came from and what I did. He explained that I had flown from Sydney and was on my own at Sister Pat's. This caused much agitation. 'Poor old bugger,' he said, 'you should have brought her down here with us. If she belonged to us we wouldn't do that to her. If she were ours we would have her here doing nothing. We would look after her. Poor old bugger!'

Boys with mandarins

We visited Tjukula again to see our beautiful waterhole among the rocks. A windmill had been installed to pump water and the surrounding area was muddy. The waterhole had become a small, inaccessible lake. Fresh signs of rabbits were obvious but it was left untouched because there was evidence of salt on the ground. It is believed that if salt is eaten with meat the animal disappears.

Further on the hunt for rabbits resumed until we came to what must surely have been the last salt lake in Western Australia, situated at the end of the Lake Amadeus Chain that stretches north of Uluru. It is magnificent, a white band against the dark foliage on the edge of the world. I asked what it was called. 'Lake Kangartu,' Lizzie's mother told me, which Lizzie laughingly said meant kangaroo piss. Naturally I had to hear the story, with the mother telling and Lizzie translating: 'See those two desert oaks in the distance? The far oak on the right is Malu, the Kangaroo. The oak in the middle distance is Euro. One day Malu the Kangaroo urinated, creating a stream of fresh, pure, running water. "Man can live forever," he said. Then Euro said "No, man has to die" and pissed into the water, turning it salty and thick, never to run free again.'

The further we drove the drier it became, with many rabbit warrens visible in the hard earth.

Lake Kangartu near Tjukula, Western Australia

They had eaten the bark on the mulgas and the remains of the trees stood stark and silver-grey in the brilliant sunshine. The women chipped away with their iron bars but could find no rabbits. It is hard to believe that such dryness can be so beautiful, the sky like an inverted blue china bowl, the mulga twisted and tortured by heat and drought.

When we returned to Tjukula other families had arrived and were sitting in small groups around their fires. A magical sight. We lit ours and had a meal, while the other families waited for the men to bring in food. They were out with their rifles on trucks, sighting animals in the beam of the headlights.

After sunset our journey continued, with sightings of groups of camels on the horizon. We had passed them on the way out along the road as well. It was the early hours of the morning when we arrived back at Docker River.

Towards evening we drove to the Petermann Ranges north of Docker River to dig for maku. We found a few goannas while we were there. They hibernate for a couple of months, making a tunnel that points down and then up, and lie in this as near to the surface as possible to absorb the warmth of the sun. Mrs Giles is the expert when it comes to catching goannas. She digs a little, then kneels down and puts her hand in the hole, issuing instructions to the girls about where to dig. Then she flattens herself on the ground, puts her arm back in the hole and springs up, hitting the goanna against an iron bar. Her speed and sureness of touch is extraordinary – the goanna is dead before you know she has it.

As the sun set the mountains seemed to come alive with colour. Lizzie pointed out a crumpled red mountain which she said was sulking, and bore the name of Muliara. According to the men's Dreaming, this mountain was an ancestor who was sulking because his wife had given him a daughter and not a son.

That night back at Docker River as I attempted to cook a baked dinner (succeeding only in burning it and attracting a few camp dogs), there was a knocking at the door. A traveller explained to Sister Pat that some people had broken down way back along the road and needed help. When she found out that

they were Aboriginal she explained that there was no cause for concern. They know the land so well and were always able to find water and food. Perhaps this was why they took such terrible risks with cars. Europeans would never survive in such conditions.

Digging for a Goanna, Petermann Ranges

The next day we took the main road to Warburton (Western Australia), turning left into Malu Road. A lengthy drive brought us to a rockhole - more a split in the rock without much water - showing signs of animals and Aboriginal stone tools. Rocky red outcrops dotted the landscape and among these someone saw a perentji (large goanna). The excitement was terrific but by the time Michael got there with his rifle the children had frightened it under the rocks. A perentji would make a meal for about fifteen people back at camp. We drove into the bush for some distance and came upon a few small trees that I had not seen before with dark green, very shiny foliage, as if they had once been part of someone's garden - an impossibility of course. There were signs of rabbits which we tracked to their burrows but with no luck. Instead we caught a goanna which was cooked for lunch. It has a unique but not unpleasant taste.

The drive home was superb, white ghost gums lining the highway past Gill Pinnacle in the Rawlinson Range. We arrived back at camp the following day and went to say goodbye. It was in uproar. A young boy had just been given a hiding for sniffing petrol and swearing. We were to bring this boy and his sister to Alice so we had to wait until the situation became calm. At last we took our leave but when we stopped to refuel at Yulara Village I discovered my case was missing. This was a catastrophe because it had everything I had brought in it, including my sketches, photographs, and even the pot of earth that I had asked permission of Lizzie's mother to take home with me. I always collect some of this red soil for its colour - so fine, like a handful of dust.

I was beginning to believe the little boy's curses were working. He had moaned to himself all the way from Docker River to Yulara Village. Someone laughed and said that everyone else had been cursed and now it was my tum. Michael decided to return to Docker so we sat and waited. He arrived just as Sister Pat was about to put the suitcase on the plane - some kind person had found it on the road - and rejoined us at Yulara at 8 pm. We got back to Alice six hours later, weary and glad to be home.

Goanna Hole

Dust, Docker River

12

MARYVALE

Michael was teaching at Titjikala School, Maryvale, where I visited him in 1986 just after the rains. The Hugh River flowed and beneath cloudy skies a world of yellow daisies appeared among the small greyish shrubs. Perfume from a white flower resembling a single stock filled the air and drifts of white appeared among the yellow. It was the same for hundreds of kilometres, people told us as they passed through. Maryvale is on the edge of the Simpson Desert, where the red sandhills begin their north–south run. One of these is so large that it appears on the map as Mt Charlotte and even it was covered with yellow daisies clambering to reach the top.

Daisies, Maryvale

Titjikala Schoolgirl, Maryvale

Tony at the Top, Maryvale

Driving south and turning left into the hills another great column of stone came into view but it was too late to explore. We boiled a billy and drank our tea among the flowers. I noticed a patch of shrubs that glistened in the sunlight. What looked like masses of tiny diamonds along its branches were droplets of clear honey deposited by ants. We sucked the sweet nectar and I remembered someone telling me that at Narwietooma there is a road leading through an avenue of mulga that appears to be covered in flowers. Again, it is honey left by ants on the tips of the leaves that sparkles like pink jewels in the sun.

I took a trip with the schoolchildren to a long line of rocks west of the school. They were learning about mountains and here we could see the backbone of a mountain washed away by an inland sea millions of years before. Of even more interest to the children was the grave of an explorer who they said had died of thirst. He cut his horse's throat and drank the blood but even that did not save him. Getting there proved to be another long drive, until at last we found a grave of stones and a headstone with the name of the German explorer on it. The stones themselves were interesting as they had the same water-worn pattern as we had seen on the river sand, relics of the inland sea. The grave was on the side of a low hill, a most sublime resting place.

We climbed the short distance to the top and I felt dizzy at the vastness of the view, the horizon

Collecting Tucker, Maryvale

a far distant circle of blue mountain ranges with hardly a break. I could only look and look. There were no daisies here. It was very dry and had a deep feeling of isolation. Back at Maryvale near the camp I saw an Aboriginal graveyard set out European style with flowers, some plastic, on the graves. The sight of it filled me with sadness.

On a subsequent visit to Maryvale I went with the women to collect wanganu grass seed. They use this to make flour for damper. The women gather the seed, gently pulling at the grass tops and shaking them into a dish. The seed has to be separated from the husks by shaking and tilting the dish until seed is on one end and husks on the other. It then has to be ground into meal by placing it on a large, flat stone and grinding it with a smaller stone. There was not enough seed for our damper. It would take many women many hours to gather enough of this fine brown seed to make a small damper. We made ours of flour, sitting around the fire eating maku and drinking tea while it cooked in the ashes.

The next day they showed me how to make necklaces from ininti beans. These are hard, shiny and either red or orange in colour. The women sat beside the fire and resharpened their piercing

Piercing Ininti Beans, Maryvale

needles, which were simple bits of wire heated and hammered to a spike. They required sharpening from time to time during the afternoon.

Each had a square of wood with four hollows carved out to hold four separate beans. At the right-hand side of the wood, at the back, was another hole. They pierced each bean with the wire, placed it over the hole and pushed the wire right through. When enough beans were pierced, the women threaded them onto string made from hair, collected and spun for the purpose. Hair is never thrown away but collected and stored for later use. The wood of the ininti tree is soft and easily carved and is used to make coolamons for displaying artefacts. Mulga, a much harder wood, is used to make boomerangs.

Special seeds were needed to put with the ininti beads and it seemed a good idea to collect some. We drove into the Simpson Desert along the Finke Road and had our evening meal just over the ridge on an enormous sandhill. The country here is an ocean of brilliant red sandhills that seem to roll on and on forever, held together by spinifex and low shrubs. The sand is soft, the texture of cornflour. Idly letting it slip through my fingers I noticed where a few particles clung together and fell they made miniature craters. These enormous sandhills are made of minute particles of white sand covered with iron oxide.

We travelled south along Chambers Pillar Road, turning right and crossing the Maryvale boundary to drive along the railway line, the boundary of Idracowra Station. The country here is red, sandy, hilly and quite rough in places. Water lay in claypans on the flat stretches among the hills. Crossing the railway line and driving west we met the main road north of Erldunda and made camp at dusk before Curtin Springs. Yulara Village again provided a shower stop, where we learned that the road was closed because of private tribal business at Docker River. This meant a drive to Uluru camp where Lizzie telephoned to get permission for us to take her through at night. Had she passed through during the day whilst such business was in progress she would have been in big trouble.

The change in plans allowed an opportunity to drive around Uluru and rest at Kata Tjuta before making camp later that evening at Tjukula. Here we discovered that all the people had gone to

Ininti Tree, Papunya

Last Light on the Sandhill, Maryvale

Warakurna to vote. We also found the brown seeds for the necklaces so plentiful beneath the nyitu bushes that we could scoop them up in handfuls.

We drove south and then west along the old Gun Barrel Highway the next day to meet the Tjukula people at Warakuma.

That night Mr and Mrs Giles and other relatives of Lizzie's joined us around our camp fire. The skin relationships of the Ngaanatjarra tribe were the main topic of conversation. Eventually only the Giles remained, telling us stories that had to be translated for me. The intonations and gestures alone were a delight. One story I remember explained how a man put all his meat (kangaroo, possum, goanna, et cetera) into his head and kept it there. The moon is his head and the dark shadows are the meat. He would send his grandson for water and while the boy was away would take out some of the meat and have it cooking on the fire when he returned. One day when the boy came

Ayers Rock (Uluru)

Gathering Ininti Beans, Papunya

back early to see his grandfather taking the meat out of his head the old man killed him. Children never look at the moon because they may be killed.

We returned to Tjukula the next morning, calling in at Giles Weather Station on our way. Tjukula has altered completely in two years. Once a small settlement of unobtrusive humpies, it was now shaping up as a town with a substantial airstrip and large areas being bulldozed for housing for the Ngaanatjarra people. Many would move from other settlements to form the community. We took the road north to Kintore, detouring into the hills to admire the vastness and the lake in the far distance. There were bushes of wild plums, small purple fruit, rich in vitamin C, and wild tomatoes (paura) in abundance, yellow-green and hard on the browning bushes which die off leaving the fruit in trails along the ground. They have a mass of black seeds in the centre that are too hot to eat.

Continuing to Kintore we found it changed too. Tents were pitched for the night and the following day an early start made along the road to Papunya, past forests of desert oaks weeping

Gathering Wild Tomatoes between Tjukula and Kintore

among the spinifex, mountains with their odd shapes and colours ranging from burnt sienna to amethyst and deepest purple. We stopped in a river bed to gather ininti beans. The trees were bare except for small tufts of new growth at the ends of their branches. Beneath them the red and orange beans glowed like jewels on the pink sand.

The road took us past magnificent Mt Liebig through Papunya, which looked deserted, as many families had moved further west. Driving slowly along Belt Range and stopping every so often to take in the breathtaking beauty, we made our way around Haasts Bluff and on to Glen Helen, across Derwent Creek. This still held some water in which giant white river gums were reflected. We turned right before Mt Sonder and drove quite a distance until stopping to walk to a gorge along a creek bed of worn river stones. On either side of the creek bed white gums formed a majestic avenue against brilliant red cliffs with warm, greyish stone sweeping in towards the centre. The shadows reached almost across the gorge as if guarding the way and, indeed, a little further on we came to a place that filled us with awe, a sacred place. White stone reached from one side to the other of a pool of water above which red rocks and white gums cast long shadows. The spirit of this place still lived but for how long? I felt a great sadness when I recalled, years before, visiting a place where the water shone like crystal and now was fouled by horses and cattle.

Driving out of the gorge we discovered that Bugger, the dog, was missing. Calling and whistling did not help. Michael went back while Lizzie drove on slowly. Still no dog, so we drove back to find Michael had vanished. The shadows were deepening as Lizzie went off to track him. I could only think of *Picnic at Hanging Rock*, it was so eerie. Little Emma and I seemed to be all that remained and then suddenly everyone appeared out of the darkness, including Bugger, and camp was made then and there on a patch of soft pink sand. The songs and chatter of birds woke us at daybreak and an early start was made back to Maryvale via the Finke River.

Haasts Bluff, Papunya

Roma Gorge

Hugh River near Maryvale

Another memorable drive took us south-east of Maryvale past the spinifex and low shrubs, desert oaks and fine, feathery ironwood trees to Yarakwatja on the Hugh River. Here again we found pink sand with stony patches and huge white river gums gnarled and shining in the sun. A bank of stone rose high above the red earth and pink sand of the river bed, red at the top and blending into a rich yellow ochre at the base. We spent the entire day here. I gathered some magnificent red and black tail feathers from the black cockatoo (iranta), the red almost exactly the same shade as the earth itself. Again we travelled home when the shadows were long and the colours vivid, stopping on the way to watch some pink-eared ducks circle three times above the water, the last time skimming the surface before coming gracefully to rest.

The Centre is home to me. My greatest joy is to camp beneath the desert oaks and listen to their sighing that ebbs and flows like the ocean, telling the sorrows of a timeless land as does the dingo's call or the wailing at camp. For a fleeting moment one is part of the Spirit of the Dreaming.

Mt Liebig

The Paintings

All works are watercolour on paper unless otherwise stated.

Page 7
Markilyi (Lizzie) 1985
71 x 50 cm
Private Collection

Page 8
*The Barwon River, Western
New South Wales* late
1950s
52 x 71 cm
Possession of the Artist

Page 10
*Chair and fire screen
embroidered in Wilcannia
colours* late 1950s
Possession of the Artist

Page 11
*Children Playing, Barwon
River* late 1950s
30.4 x 40.8 cm
Private Collection

Page 12
Combo Waterhole late 1950s
40.7 x 70.0 cm
Private Collection

Page 14
*Man of Central
Australia* c.1973
Petit point 74 x 53 cm
Possession of the Artist

Page 15
*Watching the Sports,
Yuendumu* c.1973
50.2 x 30.8 cm
Private Collection

Page 17
Wives, Yuendumu c. 1973
49 x 74 cm
Possession of the Artist

Page 19
*Barbara, Ray and Marilyn,
Beswick Station* c.1973
Petit point 40.0 x 50.5 cm
Possession of the Artist

Pages 20–21
*Road to Mt Liebig,
near Papunya* c.1978
30 x 50 cm
Private Collection

Page 22
Belt Range, Papunya c.1978
45.0 x 70.4 cm
Private Collection

Page 23
Paddlers, Papunya c.1978
40 x 50 cm
Private Collection

Page 25
Pintupi Camp, Papunya
c.1978
53 x 74 cm
Private Collection

Page 26
Napperby Crossing c.1978
15 x 20 cm
Private Collection

Page 27
Twenty-Mile, Napperby
c.1978
70 x 40 cm
Private Collection

Page 28
*River Gums, Napperby
Creek* c.1978
50 x 70 cm
Private Collection

Page 29
*Heating the Irons,
Napperby* c.1978
38 x 53 cm
Private Collection

Page 31
Napperby Stockyards c.1978
100 x 142 cm
Private Collection

Page 32
Sunset, Napperby c.1978
28 x 35 cm
Private Collection

Page 34
*Boy with Emu Chick
(Humbug)* c.1978
37x 37 cm
Private Collection

Page 35
*Gathering Berries,
Napperby* c.1978
50 x 40 cm
Private Collection

Page 36
New Trousers, Mbunghara
1981
72 x 52 cm
Private Collection

Page 38
*Mother and Child,
Napperby* c.1978
50 x 70 cm
Possession of the Artist

Page 39
Rockhole, Areyonga 1978
34 x 43 cm
Private Collection

Page 40
Mareeta's Posy 1981
50 x 31 cm
Private Collection

Page 43
Inyika, Areyonga c.1973
Petit point 74 x 52 cm
Possession of the Artist

Page 44
Mt Ziel to the South 1980
29 x 35 cm
Private Collection

Page 45
West to Mbunghara 1981
46 x 54 cm
Private Collection

Pages 46–7
Sunset, Mbunghara 1980
12 x 20 cm
Private Collection

Page 48
*The First Footprints,
Dashwood Creek* 1981
34 x 43 cm
Private Collection

Page 49
*Alison's Mug of Prultji,
Dashwood Creek* 1982
50 x 31 cm
Private Collection

Page 49
Henry, Mbunghara 1981
75 x 55 cm
Private Collection

Page 50
Canteen, Mbunghara 1987
54 x 74 cm
Private Collection

Page 51
Young Man, Mbunghara 1981
55 x 29 cm
Private Collection

Page 53
Schoolboy, Mbunghara 1980
55 x 29 cm
Private Collection

Page 55
Gabrielle Possum, Mbunghara
1981
55 x 29 cm
Private Collection

Pages 56–7
Cooking Kangaroo 1985
55 x 58 cm
Private Collection

Page 59
Markilyi (Lizzie) 1986
36 x 27 cm
Private Collection

Page 60
Waterhole, Hugh River
40.7 x 70.0 cm
Private Collection

Page 61
Mt Ooraminna 1983
50.0 x 70 cm
Private Collection

Page 62
Mountain Pass, Ooraminna
1983
40 x 140 cm
Private Collection

Page 63
Snow Daisies, Ooraminna
1983
50.0 x 70.4 cm
Private Collection

Page 64
Desert Oaks 1985
50 x 38 cm
Private Collection

Page 66
Prickly Wattle, Petermann
Ranges 1985
29 x 55 cm
Private Collection

Page 67
Rockhole at Tjilpuka 1984
52 x 37 cm
Possession of the Artist

Page 68
Tjamu and Yuntjin 1984
37 x 37 cm
Private Collection

Page 69
Grass Trees near the Border
of Western Australia,
Petermann Ranges 1984
51 x 74 cm
Possession of the Artist

Page 70
Looking for Maku,
Petermann Ranges 1985
53 x 74 cm
Possession of the Artist

Pages 72–3
Wind behind Clouds,
Petermann Ranges 1984
35 x 50 cm
Private Collection

Page 75
Papunya Range c.1978
50 x 70 cm
Private Collection

Pages 76–7
Women from Amata,
Dancing, Yirara College
Fete 1984
100 x 142 cm
Possession of the Artist

Page 79
Markilyi, Yuntjin and
Nutji Nutji (Lizzie,
Lucy and Emma) 1986
64 x 54 cm

St Stanislaus College,
Bathurst

Page 81
Lake Kangartu near Tjukula,
Western Australia 1986
53 x 74 cm
Private Collection

Page 83
Digging for a Goanna,
Petermann Ranges 1985
35 x 55 cm
Private Collection

Page 85
Dust, Docker River 1983
40 x 28 cm
Private Collection

Page 86
Daisies, Maryvale 1986
34 x 43 cm
Private Collection

Page 87
Titjikala Schoolgirl, Maryvale
1987
36 x 27 cm
Possession of the Artist

Page 88
Tony at the Top 1986
64 x 45 cm
Possession of the Artist

Page 89
Collecting Tucker, Maryvale
1986
52 x 71 cm
Possession of the Artist

Page 90
Piercing Ininti Beans,
Maryvale 1987
54 x 73 cm
Possession of the Artist

Page 91
Ininti Tree, Papunya 1987
52 x 75 cm
Possession of the Artist

Pages 92–3
Last Light on the Sandhill,
Maryvale 1986
34 x 43 cm
Possession of the Artist

Page 94
Ayers Rock c.1973
50.4 x 70.0 cm
Private Collection

Page 95
Gathering Ininti Beans,
Papunya 1987
34 x 43 cm
Possession of the Artist

Page 96
Gathering Wild Tomatoes
between Tjukula and
Kintore 1987
54 x 74 cm
Possession of the Artist

Page 97
Haasts Bluff, Papunya c.1978
40 x 50 cm
Private Collection

Page 98
Roma Gorge 1987
74 x 53 cm
Private Collection

Page 99
Hugh River near Maryvale
1987
50 x 73 cm
Private Collection

Page 100–1
Mt Liebig c.1978
40.7 x 70.0 cm
Private Collection

Index

Numbers in *italics* denote illustrations

WESTERN
AUSTRALIA

NORTHERN
TERRITORY

GIBSON

DESERT

Lake
Mackay

Nirrippi ○ Lizzie's father's
brother's country

Mt Gurner ▲ Gurner ○
Lake
Bennett

Kintore
(Wallanguru) ●

Over Dune △

Lake Macdonald

Tea & Damper (Mulga) ■

*Lizzie's and Sally's
father's country*

Lake Neale

Lake Hopkins

■ CAMP

*Lizzie's grandmother's
and grandfather's (mother's side)
country*

Docker

River

Waterhole
Quandongs

Lake
Amadeus

Christopher Lake

RAWLINSON   RANGE

Bloods

Range

Hull

Docker River

■ CAMP

River

Warakurna
○ CAMP
Giles

Tjilduka ○

PETERMANN RANGE

Giles   Creek

CAMP ▲
Kata Tjuta (the Olgas)

Yulara ▲

Uluru/Ayers

Surveyor Generals
Corner

0   50   100 km

SCALE